T0079965

HOW TO PLAY BANJO.

Tim Jumper.

EXCLUSIVELY DISTRIBUTED BY

HAL•LEONARD®

Dedicated to Bruce and Michael , who gave me my first banjo; to Neil, who showed me
how to use it; and to my students, whose need for it prompted the writing of this book.
Special thanks to Jason Shulman and Herbert Wise for their help and guidance.

Photographs
Don Kissil—page 10
John Lee—page 6
Ron Petronko—page 47
Phil Straw—page 27
Jack Tottle—page 8

Book design by Mark Stein
Cover design by Pearce Marchbank

Copyright © 1981 by Acorn Music Press.
This edition published 1988 by Amsco Publications,
A Division of Music Sales Corporation, New York, NY.

Order No. AM 35155
US International Standard Book Number: 0.8256.2205.0
UK International Standard Book Number: 0.7119.0449.9

Contents

To the Teacher

This book is designed to provide a clear and simple introduction to the five-string banjo in four playing styles—*up-picking, frailing, clawhammer,* and *bluegrass*—using the most common tuning—*open G.* The section on tuning has been located at the end of the book so that you can introduce the subject whenever you feel the student is ready for it.

I have followed a linear approach requiring mastery of each technique before proceeding to the next. The methods, examples and tunes, in their order of presentation, have proven successful with my own students over the years, but in guiding and pacing your own students' progress you may find it necessary to provide supplemental material.

Memorization is the best way to learn the written arrangements, but it is important for students to realize that playing the banjo is more than simply reading banjo music. They should be encouraged to experiment with what they learn and to try picking out tunes and variations on their own. A major goal is achieved when technique becomes a means of musical expression.

I hope that you and your students enjoy working with this book and that it helps them discover the rich tradition of the five-string banjo.

To the Student

Years ago, in colonial times, the slaves played an African instrument called a *banjar,* which looked something like a gourd drum with a wooden neck. It was strung with as many as four strings, including one short drone string. A Virginian named Joel Walker Sweeney (1810-1860) is generally credited with adding a bass string to this instrument and refining its construction, producing the five-string banjo as we know it today. The United States grew up with the lively beat and twang of the five-string banjo, and no other instrument captures so well the spirit and vitality of this country's folk music.

With this book, a good teacher, and a lot of practice, you will learn how to strum the banjo while you sing, how to pick tunes in several old-time styles, and how to play bluegrass. In the process you will also learn the words, chords and melodies of many traditional banjo tunes.

Don't be discouraged by the difficulties you may encounter. Be patient. Music is one of the most enjoyable things in life, and learning how to make music is worth all the time and effort it will take.

Accompanying a Song

Holding the Banjo

Wedge the banjo in your lap, pressing it against your chest with your right forearm. You should not support the banjo neck with your left hand. It will help to balance the instrument if you keep the neck angled up, with the peghead about level with your left shoulder.

How to Strum

Curl the fingers of your right hand into a loose fist over the strings. Flick your middle finger down so that the back of the nail brushes lightly across the first four strings. Don't hit the fifth string or use the left hand at all.

Strumming an Accompaniment

In the following song each arrow represents a strum. Sing while you strum.

Row Your Boat

G↓ ↓ ↓   ↓   ↓   ↓   ↓   ↓
Row row row your boat   Gently down the stream

↓   ↓   ↓   ↓   ↓   ↓   ↓   ↓
Merrily merrily merrily merrily   Life is but a dream

Raymond MacLain

What you are doing with the banjo is maintaining a steady beat or *rhythm* while you sing. This is called strumming an *accompaniment*.

Think of the steady beat a clock makes: tick-tock-tick-tock. That is a rhythm. Now, instead of tick-tock-tick-tock, count evenly one-two-three-four, and strum on every number or beat.

G
↓   ↓   ↓   ↓ | ↓   ↓   •   ↓   ↓   ‖
One   two   three   four | one   two   three   four
↓   ↓   ↓   ↓ | ↓   ↓   ↓   ↓   ‖
One   two   three   four | one   two   three   four

When strumming the banjo to accompany your singing you must keep a steady, even beat. Try it here.

Frere Jacques

G↓ ↓ ↓   ↓   ↓ ↓ ↓   ↓
Are you sleep - ing   Are you sleep - ing
↓   ↓ ↓   ↓ ↓ ↓
Broth - er John—   Broth - er John—
↓   ↓   ↓ ↓ ↓   ↓   ↓ ↓
Morning bells are ring - ing   Morning bells are ring - ing
↓   ↓ ↓ ↓   ↓ ↓ ↓
Ding ding dong—   ding ding dong—

Notice in both songs that you do not strum on every word, only on the beat.
Hint—To get a smooth, pleasant-sounding strum keep your hand and fingers relaxed.

Chords

A *chord* is a group of notes which sound good when played together. The G chord is played by simply strumming the strings open, that is, without touching them with the left hand fingers, since your banjo is in the *open G tuning.* Other chords will require the use of certain left hand fingers. Here is how the fingers of the left hand are named.

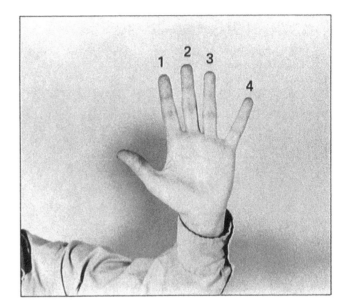

The D7 Chord

Here is a diagram of the D7 chord. It shows only four strings because the fifth string is usually not fretted.

D7

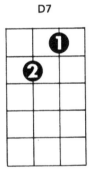

Hint—Use just the tips of your fingers on the strings and press down firmly just behind—not on— the frets. Keep your left hand nails trimmed short, otherwise they will prevent your fingertips from . properly fretting the strings.

Try strumming D7 with a steady beat.

D7

↓	↓	↓	↓		↓	↓	↓	↓	‖
One	two	three	four		one	two	three	four	
↓	↓	↓	↓		↓	↓	↓	↓	‖
One	two	three	four		one	two	three	four	

Is each string ringing clearly? Make sure each finger is touching only one string. Keep adjusting your fingers until you get a clear, ringing sound when you strum.

Changing Chords

Try this exercise using G and D7.

```
G
↓        ↓        ↓        ↓    |  ↓        ↓        ↓        ↓    |
One      two      three    four | etc.
D7
↓        ↓        ↓        ↓    |  ↓        ↓        ↓        ↓    |

G
↓        ↓        ↓        ↓    |  ↓        ↓        ↓        ↓    |

D7                                  G
↓        ↓        ↓        ↓    |  ↓        ↓        ↓        ↓    ‖
```

Keep a steady beat while changing from one chord to the other.

Watch the chord changes in this song.

Bela Fleck

Skip To My Lou

```
G↓ ↓ ↓ ↓    ↓  ↓    ↓  ↓
Skip— skip—  skip to my Lou
D7↓ ↓ ↓ ↓   ↓  ↓    ↓  ↓
Skip— skip—  skip to my Lou
G ↓ ↓ ↓ ↓   ↓  ↓    ↓  ↓
Skip— skip—  skip to my Lou
D7↓ ↓    ↓  ↓   G↓ ↓ ↓   ↓
Skip to my Lou my   dar - ling_____
```

Hint Keep your fingers over the strings while playing the G chord so that you are always ready to play D7.

Aunt Rhody

```
G↓↓ ↓  ↓     ↓  ↓↓↓
Go— tell Aunt  Rho - dy—
D7↓↓ ↓   ↓    ↓  ↓↓↓
Go— tell Aunt  Rho - dy—
G↓ ↓ ↓  ↓     ↓  ↓↓↓
Go— tell Aunt  Rho - dy—
D7↓ ↓   ↓   ↓  G↓ ↓ ↓ ↓
Old gray goose is   dead_____
```

Sore Fingers

After you have fingered a D7 chord look at your fingertips. They should have slight grooves in them from correctly fretting the strings and they might be a little sore. Don't worry, that's normal. After a few days' practice your fingertips will toughen up and the soreness will disappear.

The C Chord

While there are many songs which use just two chords there are even more which use three. Learn the C chord and you can play many of them.

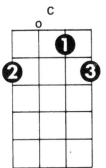

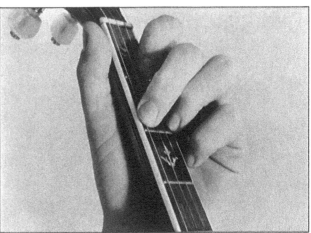

Each finger touches only one string. The third string is played open. Press down firmly and adjust your fingers until you get a good, clear sound. Because the C chord uses three fingers it will be a little harder to finger than D7. Be patient, with practice you'll get it.

C				G			
↓	↓	↓	↓	↓	↓	↓	↓
One	two	three	four	*etc.*			

C				G			
↓	↓	↓	↓	↓	↓	↓	↓

G				C			
↓	↓	↓	↓	↓	↓	↓	↓
One	two	three	four	*etc.*			

G				D7			
↓	↓	↓	↓	↓	↓	↓	↓

G				C			
↓	↓	↓	↓	↓	↓	↓	↓

D7				G			
↓	↓	↓	↓	↓	↓	↓	↓

Remember to strum evenly.

Oh Suzanna

```
G↓↓↓↓   ↓    ↓   ↓↓     ↓   ↓↓   ↓
_____I   come from Al - a -   bam - a with a
↓ ↓ ↓ ↓     D7↓↓↓ ↓
banjo on my    knee—— and I'm
G ↓   ↓   ↓   ↓     ↓   ↓↓   ↓
going to Lou - si -  an - na my——
D7↓   ↓   ↓ ↓  G↓↓↓↓
true love for to    see——
C↓↓   ↓   ↓     ↓   ↓↓   ↓
Oh—— Suz——    an - na—— now
G ↓    ↓    ↓ ↓    D7↓↓   ↓↓
don't you cry for    me—— for I
G ↓    ↓    ↓↓     ↓   ↓↓   ↓
come from Al - a -   bam - a with a
D7↓ ↓ ↓ ↓   G↓  ↓↓↓
banjo on my    knee_____
```

Round The Mountain

```
G
↓↓   ↓   ↓    ↓   ↓   ↓    ↓
     She'll be   coming 'round the
↓    ↓    ↓    ↓     ↓    ↓↓↓
mountain when she    comes
↓↓   ↓   ↓    ↓   ↓   ↓    ↓
     She'll be   coming 'round the
↓    ↓    ↓    ↓  D7↓    ↓↓↓
mountain when she    comes
↓↓   ↓    ↓ G ↓   ↓    ↓    ↓
     She'll be   coming 'round the
↓    ↓    ↓    ↓ C↓   ↓    ↓    ↓
mountain She'll be   coming 'round the
↓    ↓    ↓    ↓ G↓↓   ↓    ↓
mountain She'll be   coming 'round the
D7↓   ↓    ↓    ↓ G ↓    ↓↓↓
mountain when she    comes
```

Bill Keith

Tablature

Reading Tablature

Imagine that you are looking at the banjo facing you like this:

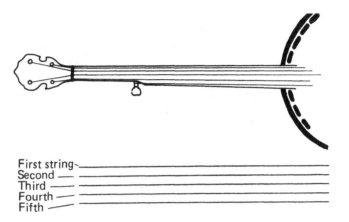

In this diagram each of the five lines represents one string of the banjo.

Numbers are written on the lines to indicate a fret to be fingered by your left hand. The line on which the number is written shows you which string to fret. A zero means that string is to be played open. This system is known as *tablature.*

First string
Second
Third
Fourth
Fifth

Picking a Tune

Below is part of a familiar tune written in tablature. Sound each string by picking up with your right index finger.

When you see this sign 𝄽 , called a *rest*, pause for one beat.

Yankee Doodle

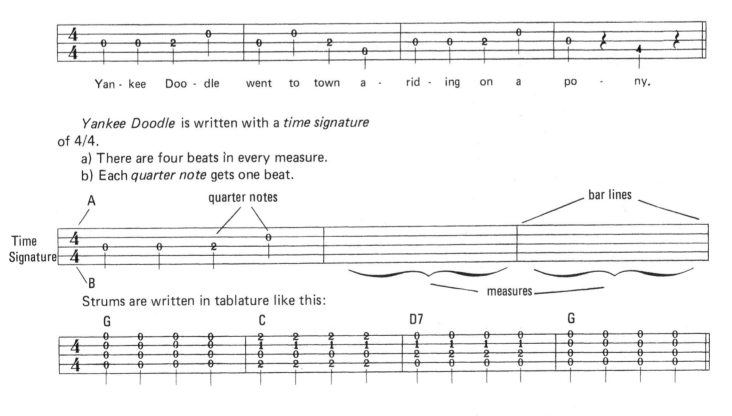

Yankee Doodle is written with a *time signature* of 4/4.

a) There are four beats in every measure.

b) Each *quarter note* gets one beat.

Strums are written in tablature like this:

Up-Picking

Up-picking is a traditional, old-time banjo style. With it you can accompany your singing in a more authentic and interesting way. This style gets its name from the fact that the single notes are sounded by picking *up* with the index finger followed by a strum as in the following example.

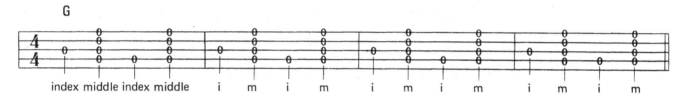

index middle index middle   i   m   i   m   i   m   i   m   i   m   i   m

Here is how the fingers of the right hand are named:

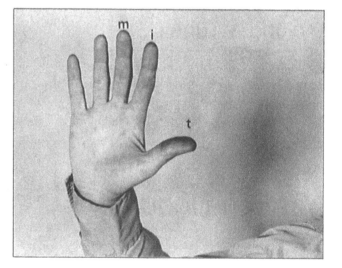

The Alternating Bass Strum

Be sure to pick the third string, then the fourth, then the third, and so on. This is the *alternating bass strum.*

Here is the same strum on the C and D7 chords.

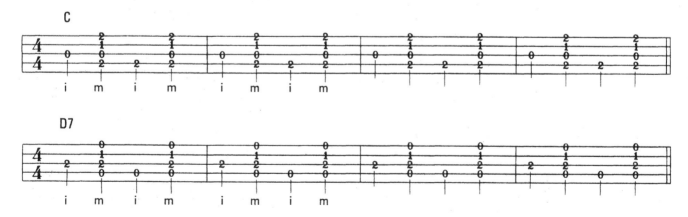

Now try using this strum to accompany a song. Remember to alternate between the third and fourth strings and to keep the beat steady.

Blue-Tail Fly

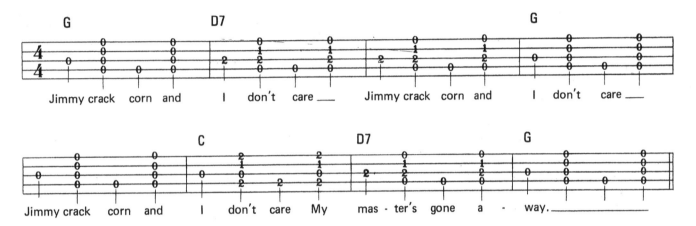

Jimmy crack corn and I don't care ___ Jimmy crack corn and I don't care ___

Jimmy crack corn and I don't care My mas - ter's gone a - way. ___

Eighth Notes

Play the following examples. There are four beats in each measure. The notes whose stems are connected are called *eighth notes.* Two eighth notes equal one quarter note—therefore one eighth note gets one half beat. You play two eighth notes in the time it takes you to play one quarter note.

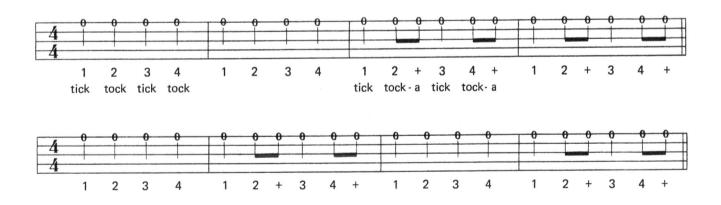

The Basic Banjo Beat

In the next example the strum is followed by a note on the fifth string. Use your thumb to pick the fifth string.

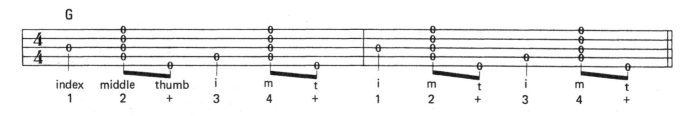

It is very important that you maintain the correct rhythm of a quarter note followed by two eighth notes. When done properly this strum gives you that bright, bouncy sound unique to the five-string banjo.

Try the same strum with the C and D7 chords.

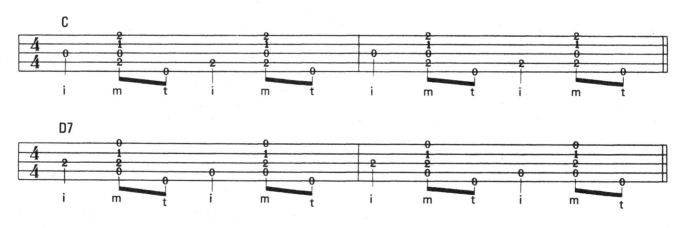

Don't look at your right hand while you strum. Keep your eyes on the tablature as much as possible. Let your fingers find the strings.

Once you feel comfortable with this strum, use it with these songs.

Crawdad

You get a line _____ I'll get a pole _____ hon - ey _____

You get a line _____ I'll get a pole _____ babe _____

You get a line _____ I'll get a pole _____ We'll go ___ down to the craw - dad ___ hole _____

Hon - ey _____ oh ___ su - gar ba - by ___ mine. _____

The Marching Saints

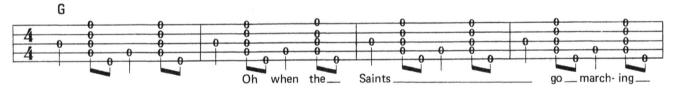

Oh when the ___ Saints _____ go ___ march- ing ___

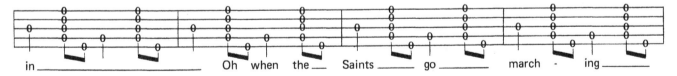

in _____ Oh when the ___ Saints _____ go _____ march - ing _____

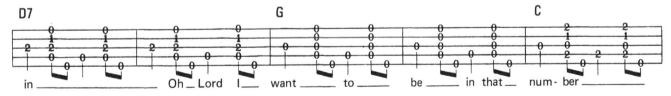

in _____ Oh ___ Lord I ___ want _____ to _____ be _____ in that ___ num - ber _____

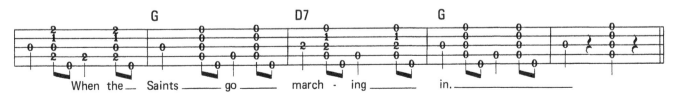

When the ___ Saints _____ go _____ march - ing _____ in. _____

Playing Solos

The banjo is a fine accompaniment instrument, but it can also be used to play tunes or melodies. This is called playing a *solo.*

Picking Melody Notes

When playing solos you will continue to use the up-picking strum, but you must be able to pick any of the first four strings with your index finger. This is very important because the strings you pick will be the melody notes of the tune.

In the following exercises be sure you are picking the correct strings. Keep your eyes on the music as much as possible.

First Solo

Here is a familiar tune for your first solo.

Even though this is a banjo solo the words have been included in case you feel like singing along.

Goodnight, Ladies

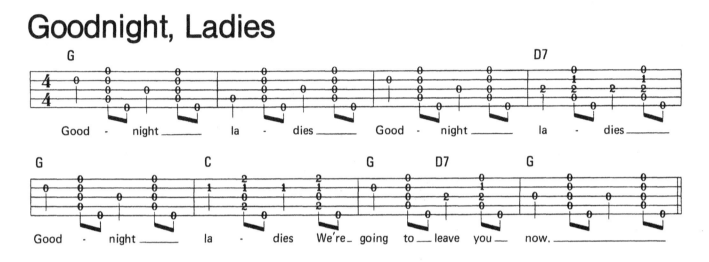

Here's an old square dance tune. Give it a try.

Boil 'Em Cabbage Down

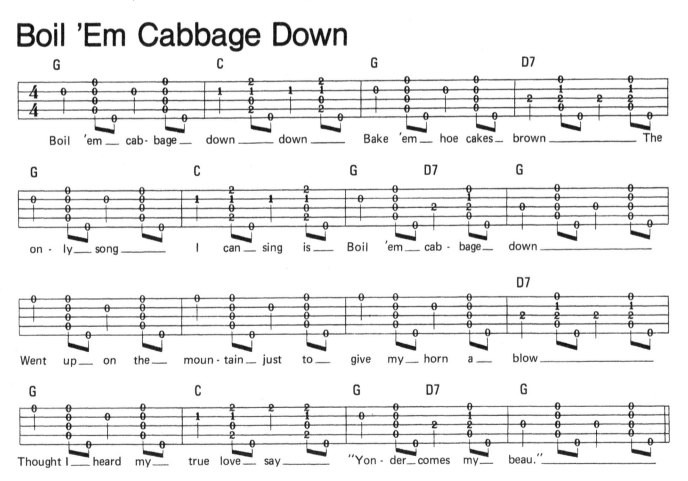

Hint—Begin building a repertoire by memorizing this tune. It's more fun to play not having to read the music from the book.

Other Tunes

Often the melody of a song will require you to play several single notes in a row without any strums in between.

In the following song watch for where you strum and where you don't. Try singing along. You'll find it very helpful for playing the rhythm accurately.

Hard Ain't It Hard

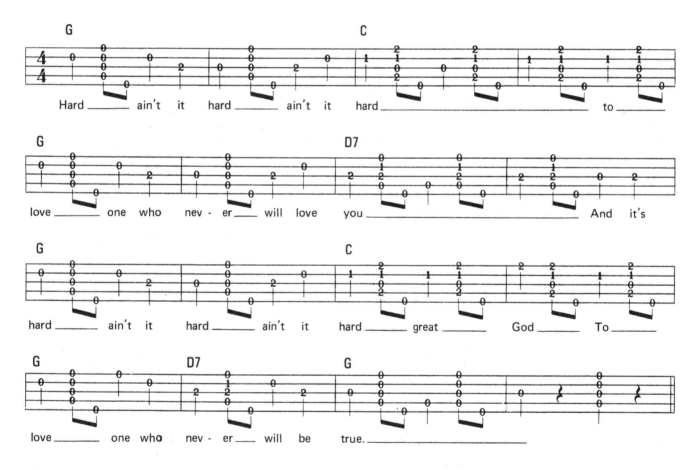

Hint—When I am learning a tune I find it is helpful to practice the difficult parts separately until I get them smoothed out. Then I go back and play the entire tune watching out for the trouble spots.

Here is the well-known outlaw ballad, *Jesse James.*

Jesse James

Hint—It's better to play tunes slowly but evenly when first learning them. Your ability to play faster will develop with time and practice.

Left Hand Techniques

Hammering-on

Hammering-on is another method of fretting a string which will add variety to your playing. Here is what it looks like in tablature.

Pick the fourth string, and, while it is still sounding, hammer it with the second finger of your left hand at the second fret, hard enough to actually sound another note. The harder you hammer, the louder the second note will be.

You can hammer-on with any finger on any string and on any fret, as in the following examples.

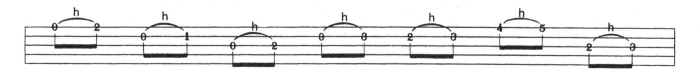

Notice where hammering-on is used in this song.

Tom Dooley

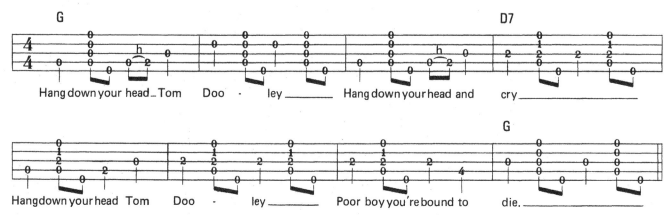

Hang down your head _ Tom Doo - ley _____ Hang down your head and cry _____

Hang down your head Tom Doo - ley _____ Poor boy you're bound to die. _____

Adding a Strum

Immediately after hammering-on add a strum and a fifth string note. This will produce a series of eighth notes.

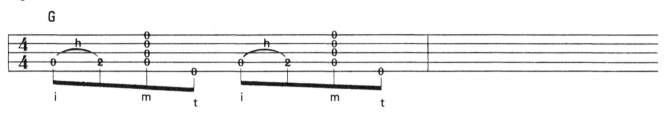

Hint—After hammering, lift the second finger off the fourth string to get ready for the next hammer.

Now try this exercise making sure you hold the quarter note one full beat.

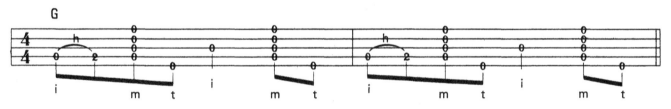

This is a basic banjo sound. Play it over and over until you can do it with a steady beat. It may take a while for your hammering finger to get strong enough to produce a good clear note. Don't give up, just keep on hammering.

Hammering-on C and D7

When doing a hammer, lift only your hammering finger; leave the other fingers on the chord.

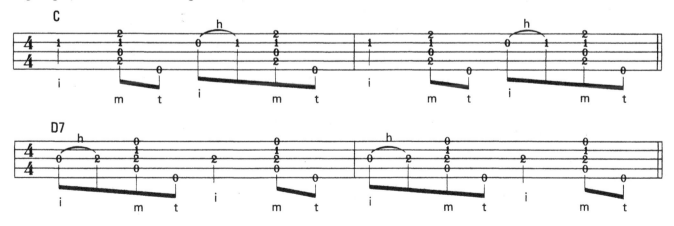

Hammering-on is used in a tune for two purposes: as a way of varying the rhythm, and as a way of adding extra notes needed for the melody.

Lynchburg Town

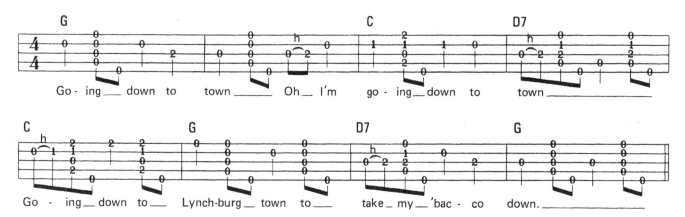

Johnnie Booker

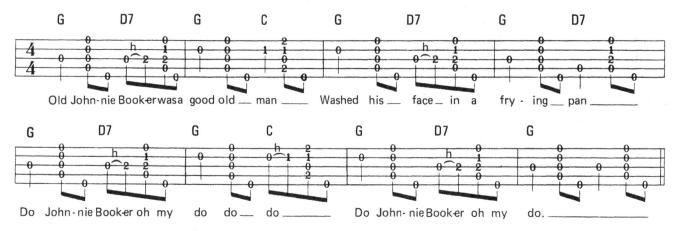

Hint—Memorizing a tune will help you play it better and it adds to your playing repertoire. Remember to sing along.

Pulling-off

Pulling-off is just the opposite of hammering-on. It is written like this.

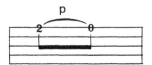

Put your second finger on the second fret of the first string and pick the first string with your index finger. While the string is still sounding, pull your second finger off the string with a plucking motion, lifting your finger and at the same time pulling it to the side. This will make the open first string sound.

As with hammer-ons, you can pull-off using any finger on any string on any fret. For example:

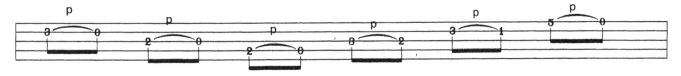

Notice the pulling-off in this tune.

Pickin' And Grinnin' #1

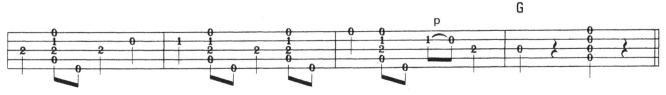

Pulling-off is used for the same purposes as hammering-on: to vary the rhythm and to add notes needed in the melody.

Sourwood Mountain

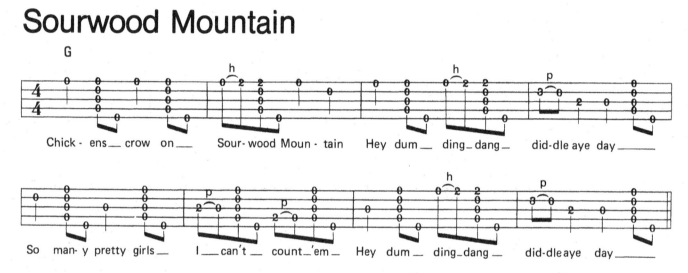

Chick - ens __ crow on __ Sour-wood Moun - tain Hey dum __ ding_dang __ did-dle aye day_____

So man- y pretty girls __ I __ can't __ count __'em __ Hey dum __ ding_dang __ did-dle aye day_____

Little Birdie

Lit - tle Bir - die _____ Lit - tle Bir - die _____ Come __

sing _____ to __ me _____ your __ song _____ Got a

short _____ time _____ for __ to stay _____ here _____ And a __

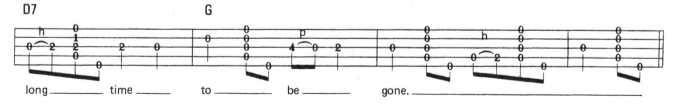

long _____ time _____ to __ be _____ gone. _____

The Em Chord

A small *m* after a chord stands for the word *minor.* Minor chords have a characteristically darker sound than major chords. Strum the Em chord and compare its sound with that of the other chords you know.

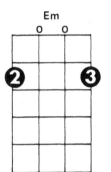

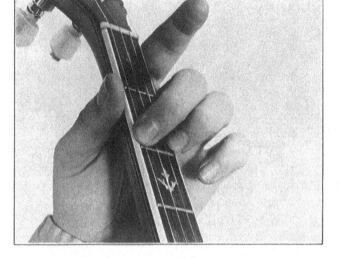

Notice the interesting contrast Em provides to G in the first line of *Sally Ann.*

Sally Ann

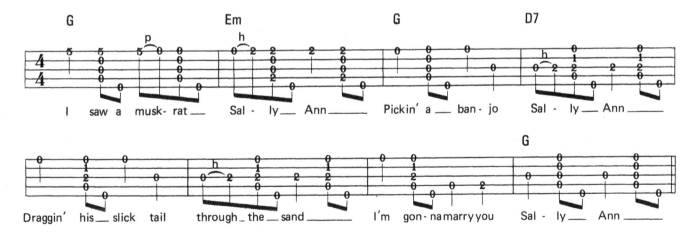

Slides

As you might guess from the name, a *slide* is done by moving a finger up or down a string from one fret to another. Here is a common example.

Place the second finger of your left hand on the third string at the second fret. Pick the string with your index finger and while the string is still sounding slide your finger up to the fourth fret without releasing the pressure on the string. This will make the string sound the fourth fret note.

Keep pressing down on the string while you slide your finger, otherwise the string will stop vibrating and you won't hear any sound at all. Don't slide too fast; each note is a full eighth note. You should hear each note clearly.

Now try this. Remember to take your finger off in time to play the open third string.

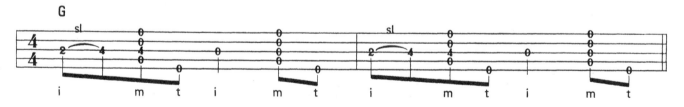

Slides are used for the same purposes as hammering-on and pulling-off.

The next tune is a favorite of banjo pickers. Because it was intended to be used for square-dancing it is made up of two short sections, labeled A and B. The dots at the end of each section mean you are to repeat that section. Play the A section twice, then the B section twice, over and over as long as you like.

Cripple Creek

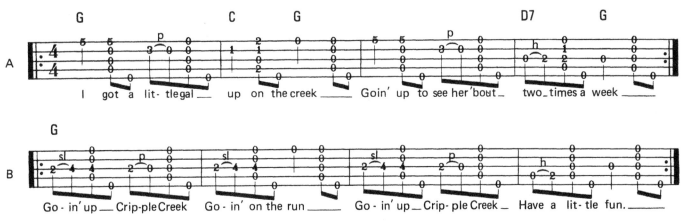

I got a lit- tle gal __ up on the creek _____ Goin' up to see her 'bout __ two __ times a week _____

Go - in' up __ Crip-ple Creek   Go - in' on the run _____   Go - in' up __ Crip - ple Creek __   Have a lit - tle fun. _____

Once you can play *Cripple Creek* with a lively beat and a clear sound on all the hammers, slides and pulls, you have mastered the basics of good five-string banjo playing.

The F Chord

The F chord uses all four fingers so it may take a while to master.

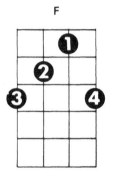

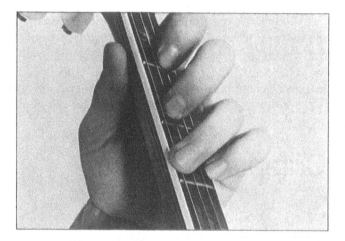

Listen to the *old-time* sound of the F chord in the next song.

Old Joe Clark

Old Joe Clark he had a mule Name was Morgan Brown

Ev - 'ry tooth in that mule's head Was six - teen inch - es round

Fare thee well Old Joe Clark Fare Thee well I say

Fare thee well Old Joe Clark I'm bound to go a - way.

Bar Chords

When the banjo is tuned to open G, fretting all the strings with your first finger at any fret will produce a chord. This is called *barring.* Notice the position of the hand in these photographs.

When playing a bar chord, the wrist curves more and the thumb is lower on the neck. This allows you to keep your finger flat against the fingerboard.

With your hand and fingers in this position, bar the fifth fret, keeping the thumb on the neck directly behind the first finger, and the finger parallel and close to the fret. Squeeze firmly and strum. All the strings should ring clearly.

Barring the fifth fret is another way of playing a C chord. To distinguish this from the first C chord you learned it will be referred to as C-v, that is, C barred at the fifth fret. Watch for it in the next two songs.

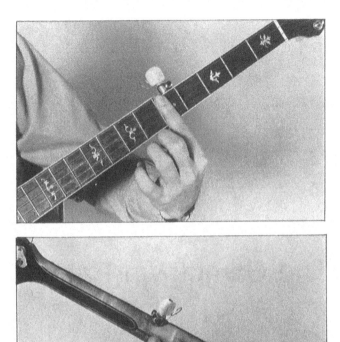

CV

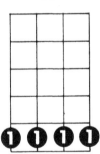

Wildwood Flower

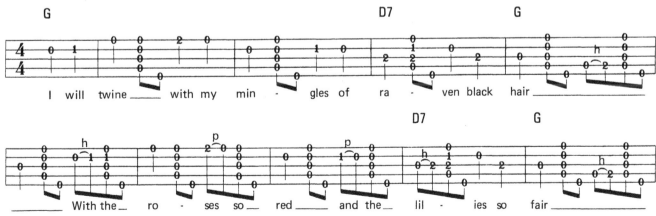

I will twine___ with my min - gles of ra - ven black hair___

___ With the_ ro - ses so_ red___ and the_ lil - ies so fair___

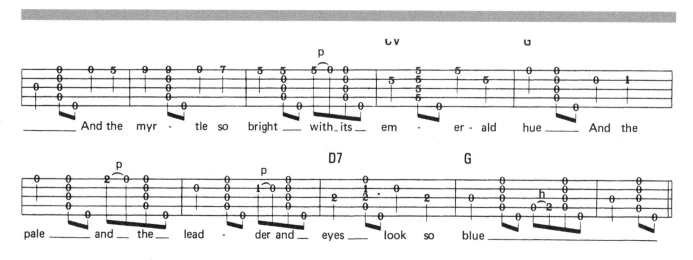

CV   G

_____ And the myr - tle so bright ___ with_its___ em - er - ald hue _____ And the

pale _____ and _ the__ lead - der and _ eyes ___ look so blue _____

The Camptown Races

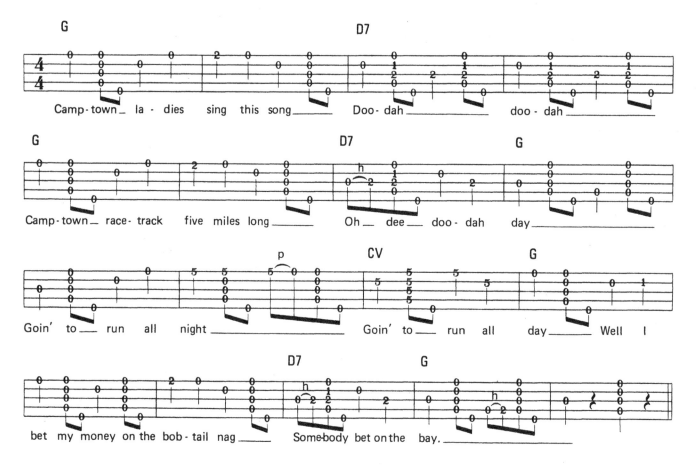

Camp - town_ la - dies sing this song_____ Doo - dah _____ doo - dah _____

Camp - town_ race - track five miles long_____ Oh _ dee _ doo - dah day_____

Goin' to _ run all night _____ Goin' to _ run all day_____ Well I

bet my money on the bob - tail nag_____ Some-body bet on the bay. _____

Another Rhythm

The following example is written with a time signature of 3/4.

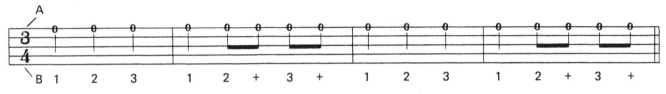

a) There are three beats in every measure.

b) Each quarter note gets one beat; each eighth note gets one-half beat.

Accompaniment in $\frac{3}{4}$

This is the alternating-bass accompaniment pattern for songs in 3/4 time. Play it over and over until you get the swing of it and then trying using it with the next song.

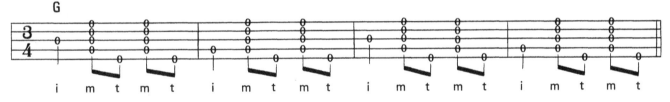

Old Smokey

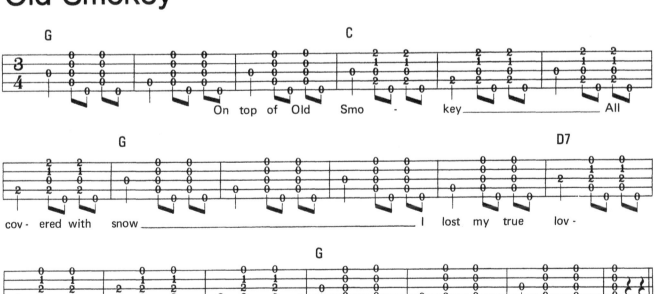

Solos in $\frac{3}{4}$ Time

Here are two solo arrangements in 3/4 time. Try for a smooth, swinging rhythm, stressing the first beat of each measure.

Down In The Valley

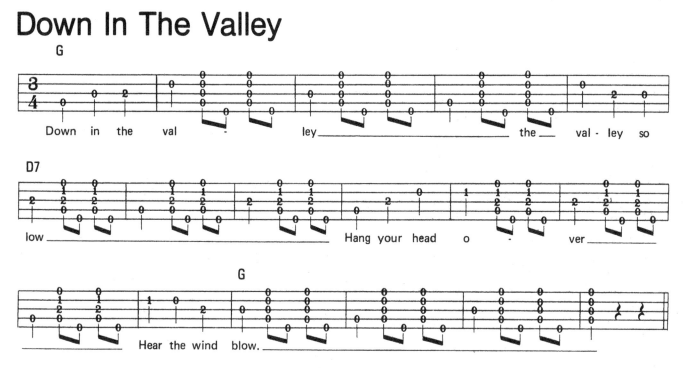

Brown Eyes

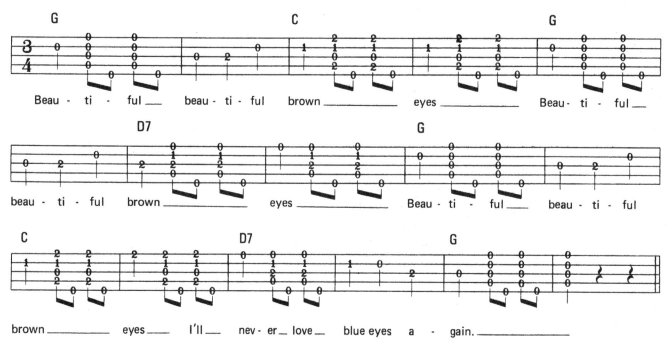

The Key of C

Songs which use the chords G, C, and D7, with G as the main chord, are said to be in the *key of G*. Songs in the *key of C* use the chords C, F, and G7, with C as the main chord.

Here is the G7 chord.

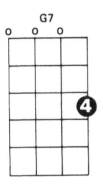

Compare the sound of the following exercises.

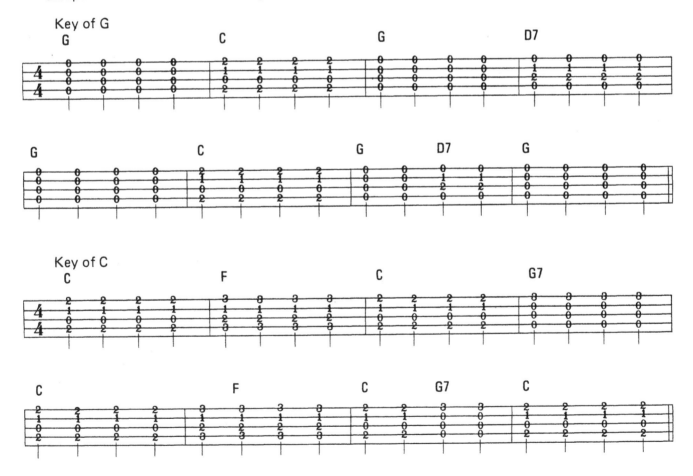

There are twelve keys in music. G and C are the most useful for the banjo since they are the easiest to play in.

Here are a couple of songs in the key of C.

Johnnie Booker

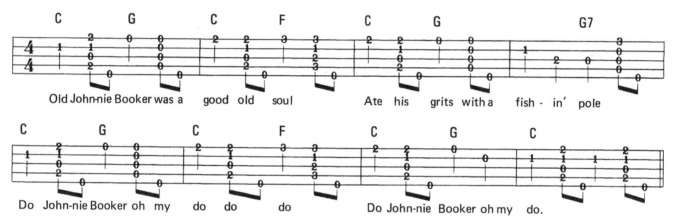

The Wabash Cannonball

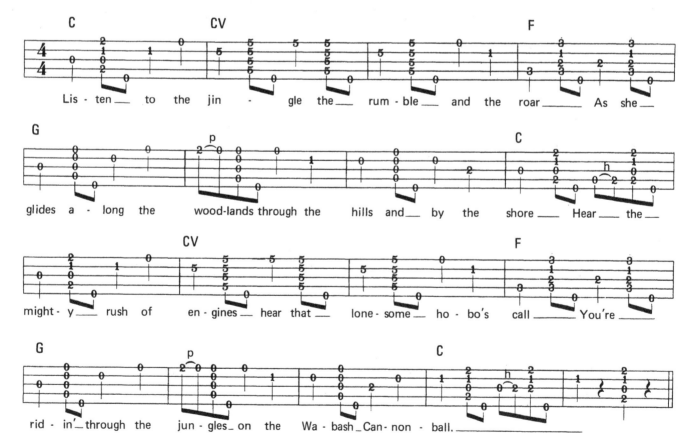

Frailing

Another traditional banjo style even more versatile than up-picking is called *down-picking* or more commonly, *frailing.* Frailing is just like up-picking except you pick the melody notes *down* with your *middle* finger, using the back of your nail to sound the string. Once you can do it you will find that it is even easier than up-picking.

The Frailing Stroke

Hold your hand in a claw-like position over the strings with your middle finger extended a little beyond the others.

Pick the first string with the back of the middle fingernail using a motion from the wrist and forearm as if you were rapping on a table. The hand moves *down*—toward the floor—and *in*—toward the banjo head. Don't flick the middle finger out. Maintain the claw position and on the follow-through let the middle fingernail actually hit the banjo head after sounding the first string.

Having picked the first string, your hand should seem to bounce off the banjo head to be in position for the strum. The basic frailing rhythm is exactly the same as that of up-picking.

Play this over and over until you get a good clear sound with an even steady beat.

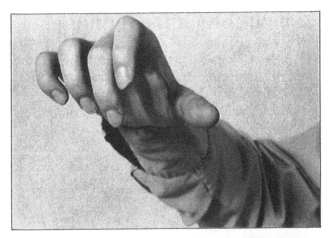

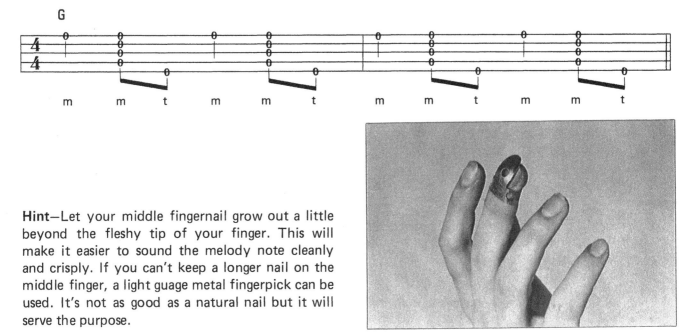

Hint—Let your middle fingernail grow out a little beyond the fleshy tip of your finger. This will make it easier to sound the melody note cleanly and crisply. If you can't keep a longer nail on the middle finger, a light guage metal fingerpick can be used. It's not as good as a natural nail but it will serve the purpose.

Frailing the Other Strings

Using the same right hand motion try picking down on the second string. Your middle fingernail will briefly contact the first string, not sounding it but bouncing off it to prepare for the strum which follows.

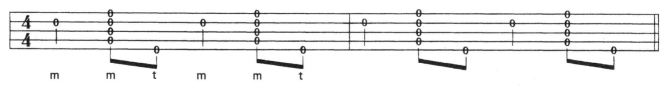

When picking the third string, your nail will bounce off the second string.

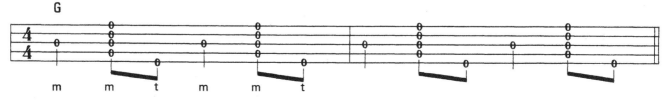

When picking the fourth string, your nail will bounce off the third string.

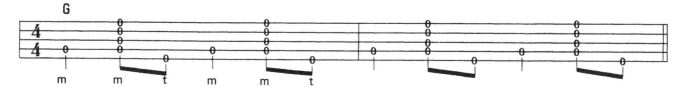

This is the trickiest part of frailing. Be patient. Remember, anyone who plays the banjo has experienced at one time the same difficulties you are facing now.

Here is one of your old up-picking exercises. Play it with the frailing stroke. Work for a clear sound and a steady beat.

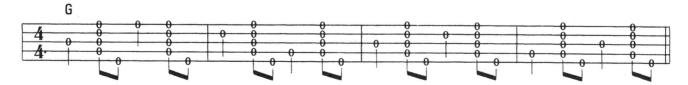

Here are a couple of new tunes to try in the frailing style.

Buffalo Gals

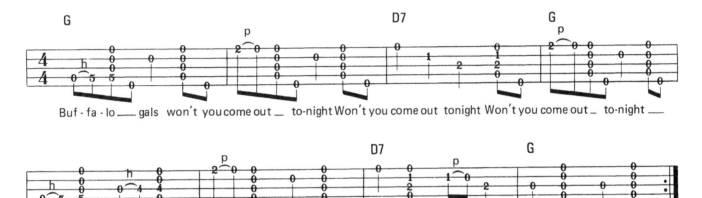

Buf - fa - lo __ gals won't you come out __ to-night Won't you come out tonight Won't you come out __ to-night __

Buf - fa- lo __ Gals won't you come out __ to-night And __ dance by the light of the moon._____

Waterbound

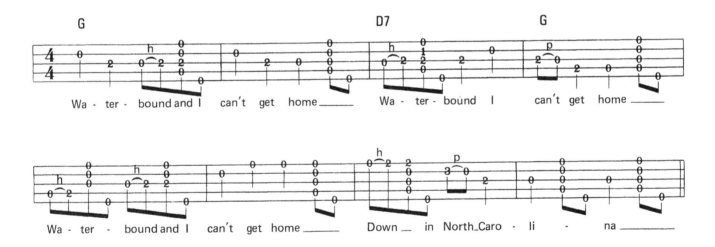

Wa - ter - bound and I can't get home_____ Wa - ter - bound I can't get home_____

Wa - ter - bound and I can't get home_____ Down __ in North_Caro - li - na _____

Since the rhythms and all the left-hand techniques you learned in up-picking are exactly the same in frailing, you can now go back and play any of the tunes in the book with the frailing stroke. Frailing produces a crisper sound and more rhythmic drive than up-picking. You will also discover that as your frailing technique improves you can play faster and more accurately.

Right Hand Techniques

The Fifth String

So far you have been picking the fifth string after every strum. It's good, however, to leave out the fifth string note once in a while so as to avoid playing the same sound and the same beat measure after measure, which can get tedious.

Notice the different beats in the following exercises.

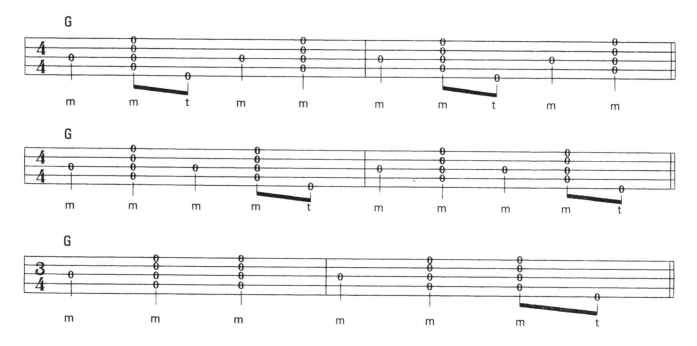

Watch for where the fifth string is not picked in the next tune.

Flop-Eared Mule

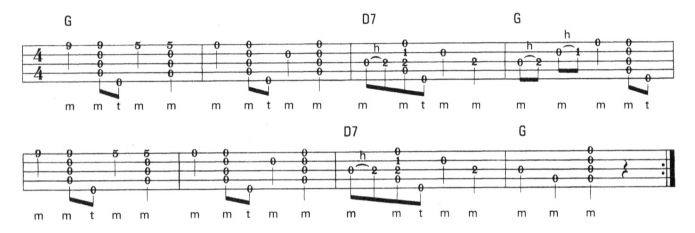

Go back to some of the tunes you've already learned and try playing them, leaving out some of the fifth string notes.

Double-Thumbing

You have seen how using the fifth string less enables you to play different rhythms. Using the fifth string more will achieve similar results. This is called *double-thumbing.*

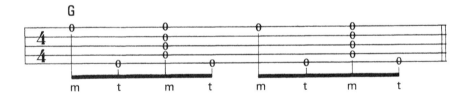

a) Frail the first string with your middle finger.
b) Pick the fifth string with your thumb
c) Strum down with your middle finger.
d) Pick the fifth string again.
All the notes are eighth notes.

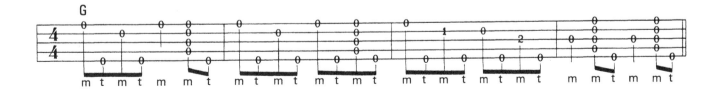

Notice how double-thumbing adds a lively sound to this tune.

Goin' Down The Road Feelin' Bad

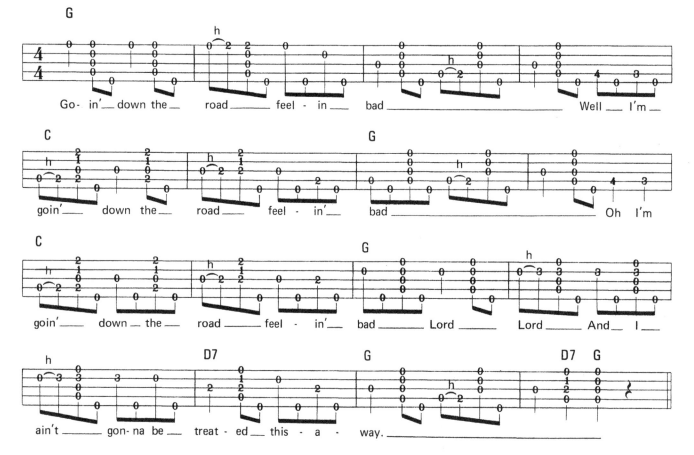

Try double-thumbing in some of the other tunes you have learned.

Drop-Thumbing

Drop-thumbing is a right-hand technique which will add a different accent to the basic frailing rhythms.

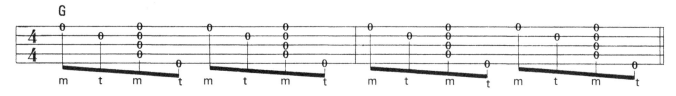

a) Frail the first string.
b) Drop your thumb down to pick the second string.
c) Strum down with your middle finger.
d) Bring your thumb back up to pick the fifth string.

All the notes are eighth notes.

Notice the rippling effect drop-thumbing adds to the following tunes.

Pickin' And Grinnin' #2

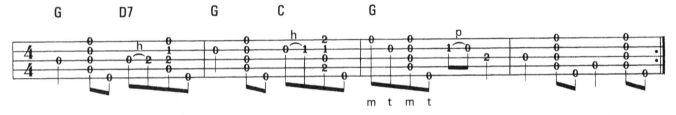

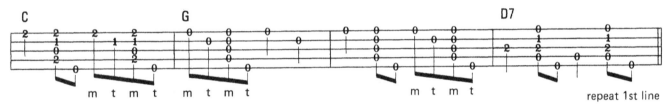

Irish Melody

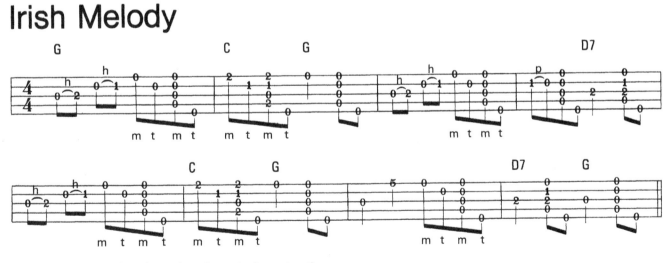

Try adding the drop-thumb technique to the other songs you have learned.

Hint—Old-time banjo pickers achieve their smooth, flowing sound by constantly replaying the tunes in their repertoire. They play a lot simply because they enjoy the music. Play over the pieces you have already learned. Not only will you find it enjoyable, but your playing will improve quickly.

Clawhammer

A more refined type of frailing is known variously as *drop-thumb frailing, melodic frailing, strumless frailing,* or simply, *clawhammer.* The differences between frailing and clawhammer are subtle but unmistakeable once your ear is attuned to them. In frailing the melody generally alternates with chords, i.e. strums, whereas in clawhammer the emphasis is on linear melody with few chord-strums. The following examples point out the main differences between the two styles.

In clawhammer fewer strums are used.

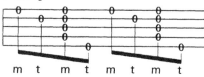

Clawhammer uses more varieties of drop-thumbing.

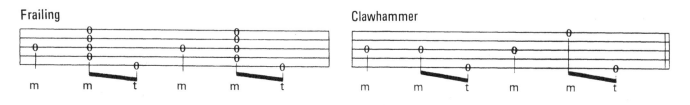

Clawhammer frequently uses drop-thumbing instead of pulling-off.

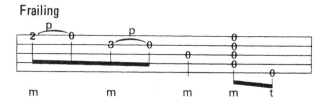

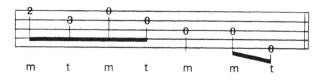

In clawhammer the fifth string is often used as a melody note. Notice also that it is a quarter note.

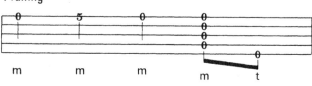

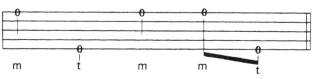

June Apple

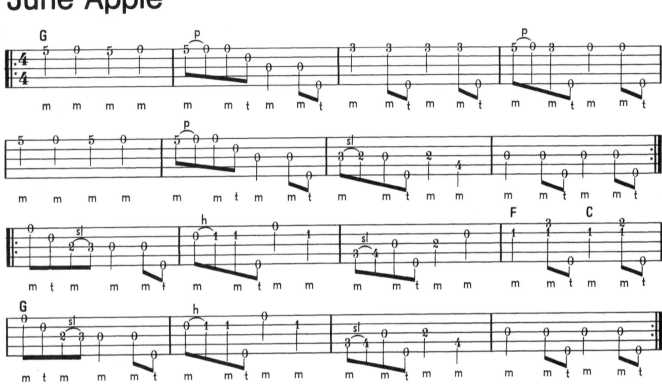

Sandy River Belle

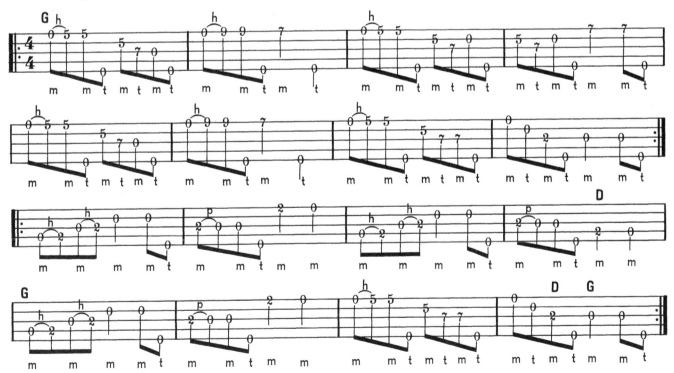

The D Chord

The second section of *Nancy Rowland* calls for a D chord. Here it is.

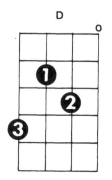

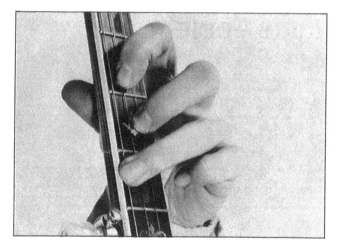

Nancy Rowland

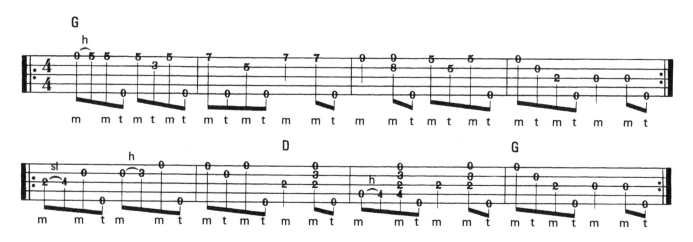

Further Study

For a more detailed description of the claw-hammer style and a fine collection of traditional tunes, see Miles Krassen's *Clawhammer Banjo,* Oak Publications.

Bluegrass

Bluegrass is a much more intricate and rhythmically complex style than the old-time ones you have learned. It is sometimes called *three-finger picking* or *Scruggs style.* Whatever name it goes by, the bluegrass sound is unique and distinctive.

Picks

First of all get yourself a thumb pick—small, medium, or large, depending on the size of your thumb—and two metal finger picks—the kind with holes in them.

The thumb pick should fit snugly enough not to slip around when you play.

The finger picks are put on your index and middle fingers, and may be bent to fit the size and shape of your fingertips.

Wear the picks whenever playing bluegrass; you'll soon get used to the feel of them.

Right Hand Position

The correct right hand position is essential to good bluegrass banjo playing. Support your right hand by resting your ring finger or your little finger—or both—on the head of the banjo, below the strings a little to the left of the bridge.

Curl your index and middle fingers into a claw-like position over the strings; your middle finger over the first string, your index finger over the second string. Your thumb should be over the fifth string, extended slightly ahead of the fingers like a hitchhiker's.

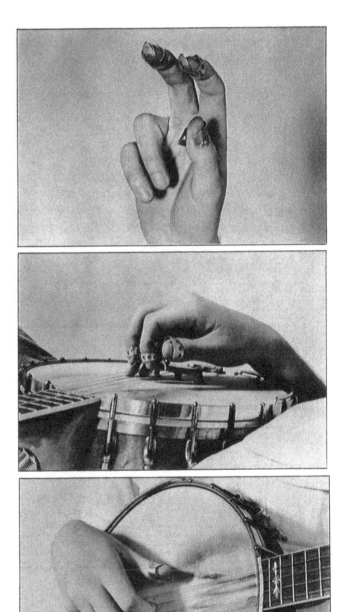

Concentrate on maintaining the correct right hand position while you try this exercise a few times.

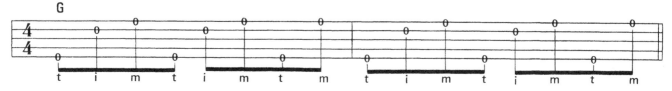

Are you getting a clear sound from each string? All the notes are eighth notes and, when correctly played, produce an even-sounding *roll,* or flow of notes which is the essence of the bluegrass sound.

Rolls

A roll is a series of notes picked by the right hand fingers in a recognizable pattern. Mastery of the basic rolls is the foundation of bluegrass banjo playing. The one you just played is called a *forward roll.* Here are two others, called *reverse rolls.*

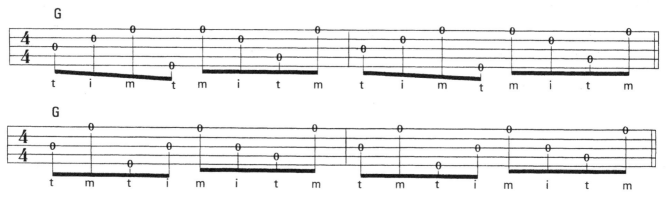

Notice how these same two rolls can be used to pick a different combination of strings.

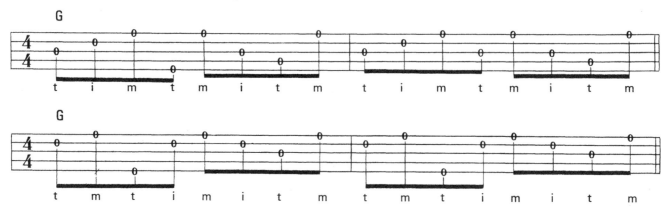

Try playing these rolls with the C and D7 chords. Aim for a clear, flowing sound. Don't worry about speed right now. Concentrate on accuracy and keeping the beat. Speed will come naturally with practice.

Hint—When playing, don't let your thumb drift back toward your palm and fingers. Maintain the correct right hand position. It will aid your progress.

A Bluegrass Solo

Here is a tune in the bluegrass style using the rolls you have learned. Most of the melody notes in a bluegrass solo are picked by the thumb, so stress the thumb notes, except for those on the fifth string.

Earl Scruggs

Worried Man Blues

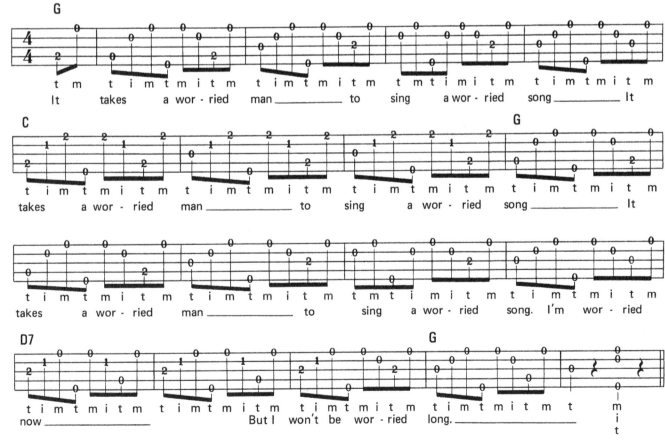

More Rolls

Here are some other common rolls. Try them with C and D7 as well as G, and don't be afraid to experiment with various string combinations.

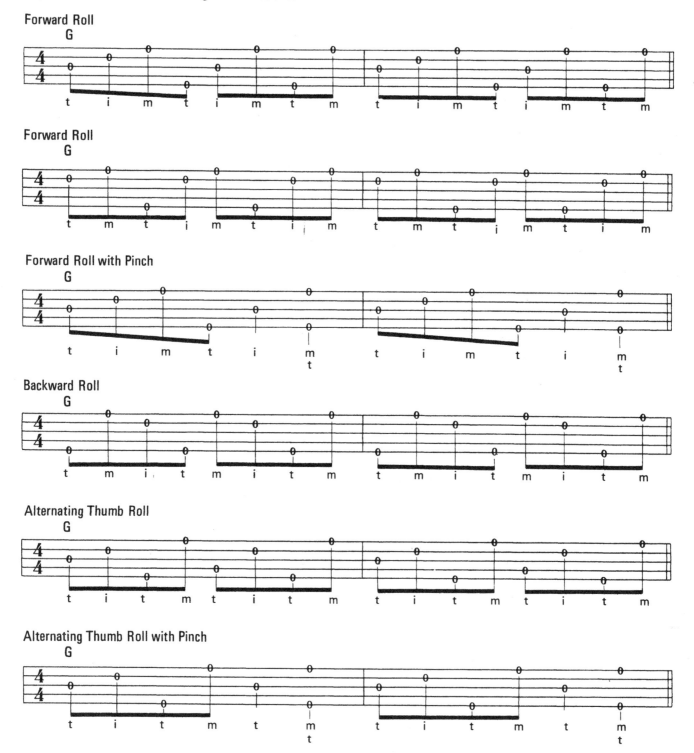

Look for the various rolls in the next tunes.

Will The Circle Be Unbroken

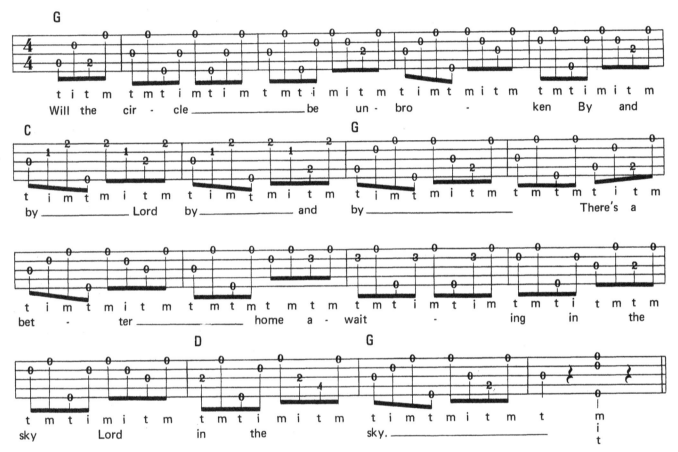

Roll In My Sweet Baby's Arms

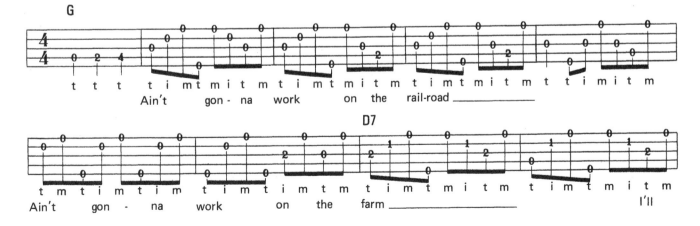

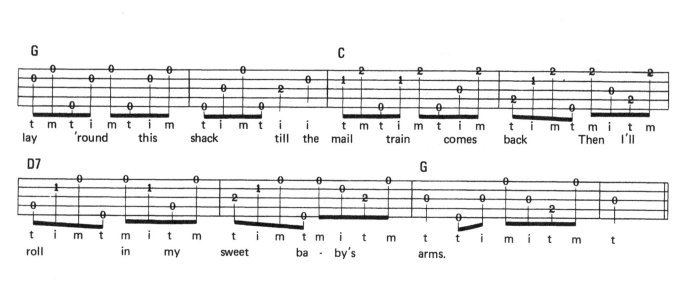

lay 'round this shack till the mail train comes back Then I'll
roll in my sweet ba - by's arms.

Licks

A *lick* is a right hand roll combined with a left hand technique—hammer, pull, or slide.

Here is a short slide combined with a reverse roll.

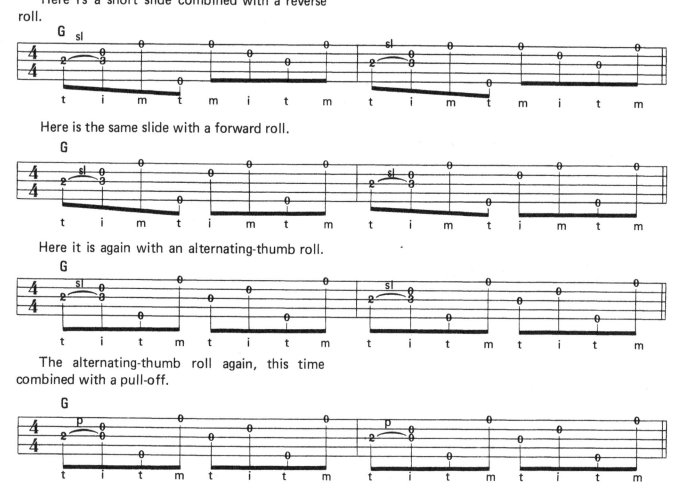

Here is the same slide with a forward roll.

Here it is again with an alternating-thumb roll.

The alternating-thumb roll again, this time combined with a pull-off.

The same roll with a hammer-on.

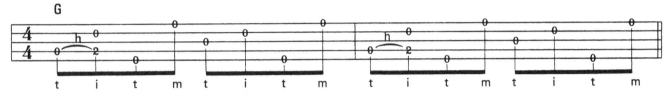

Hint—If a lick seems particularly difficult, practice the roll by itself on open strings. When you have the roll down, simply add the left hand technique to it.

Cripple Creek

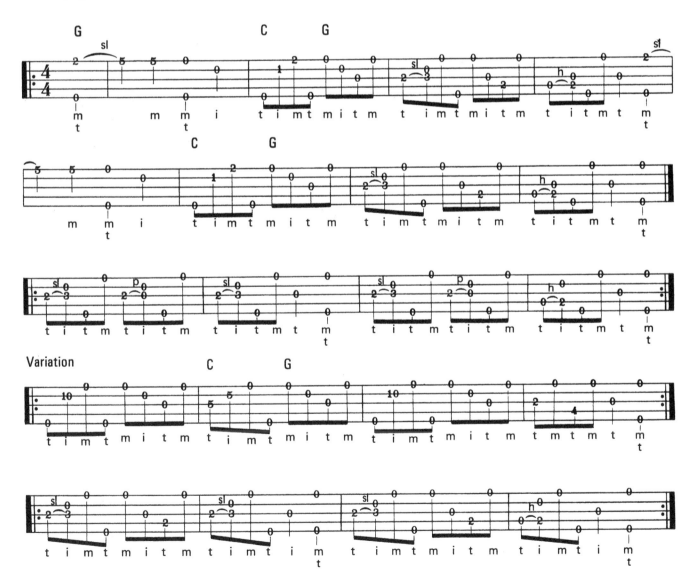

Variation

Other Licks

Here are some other standard bluegrass licks.
Notice which rolls are being used.

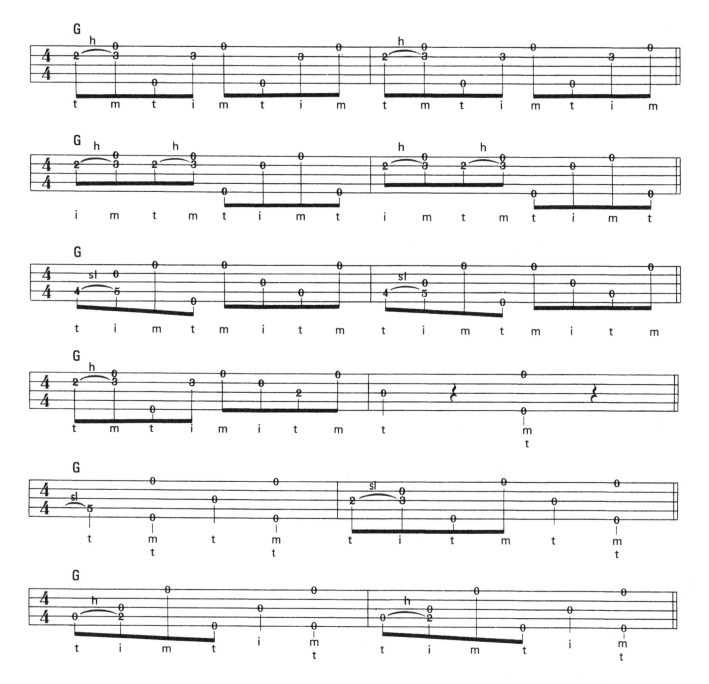

Add these tunes to your repertoire.

Ground Hog

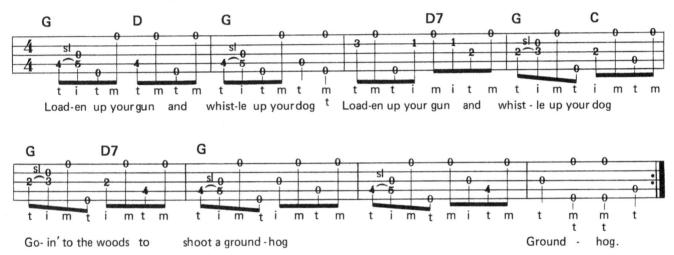

Down The Road

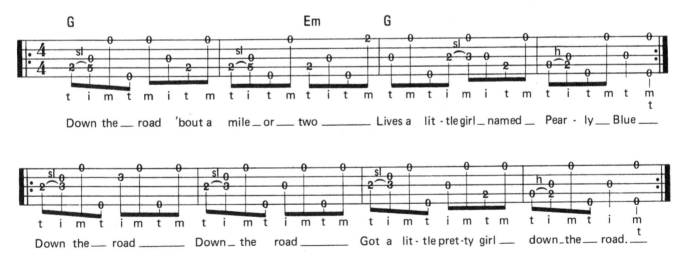

Starts and Finishes

There are certain licks which have become traditional beginnings and endings of bluegrass tunes. Here are a few of the most common ones. The symbol ⁷ is an *eighth rest*. It tells you to pause for half a beat.

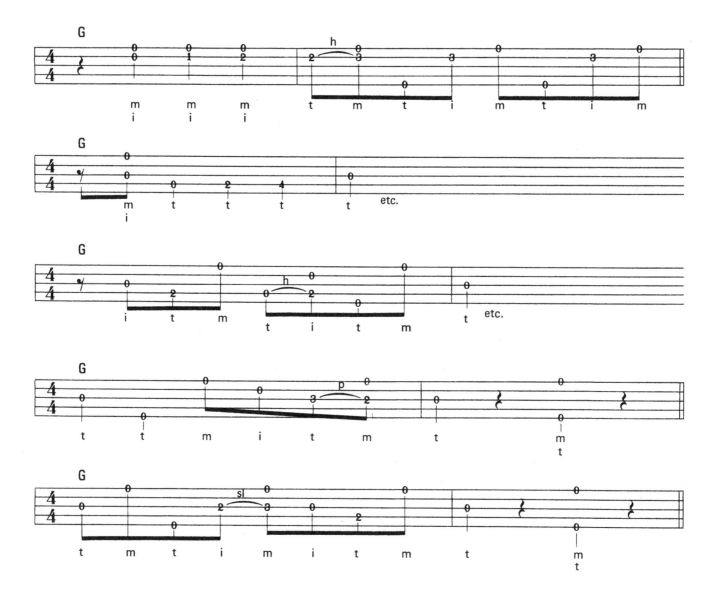

A *tag ending* is a phrase adding on to the actual ending of a tune. The most commonly used tag in bluegrass music is the familiar "shave and a haircut—two bits." Here are some variations on that theme.

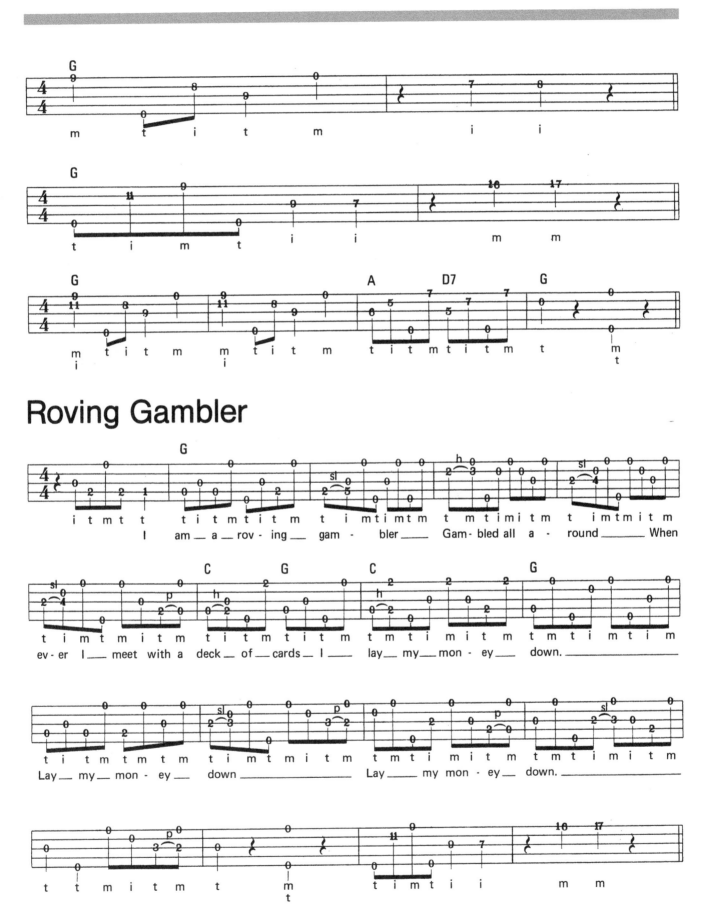

Roving Gambler

Careless Love

Sally Goodin

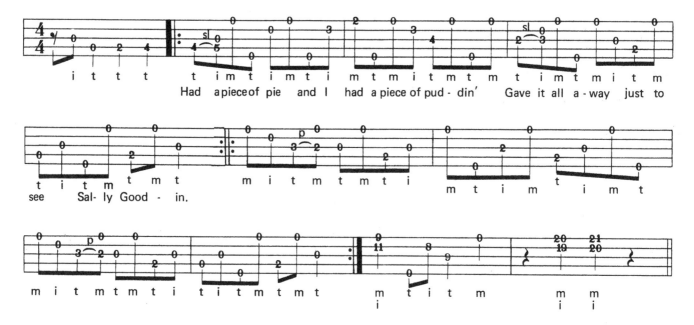

Tuning

Tuning to a Piano

If a piano is available you can tune your banjo to it with the aid of the following diagram. In the open G tuning the strings are tuned to these notes, beginning with the fifth string: G D G B D.

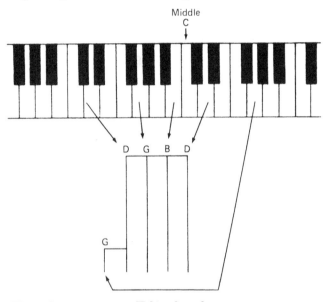

Tuning to a Pitchpipe

The notes of a pitchpipe sound one octave higher than the open strings. Have your teacher explain how to use one.

A *pitchpipe* is a set of five small tubes containing harmonica-type reeds.

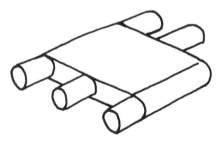

Tuning the Banjo to Itself

This is a method of tuning the banjo to itself—you don't need a piano or a pitchpipe.

For the purposes of getting in tune, assume that the fourth string is correct, as long as it is not so loose that it buzzes against the frets, nor so tight that it is difficult to press down.

Finger the fourth string at the fifth fret and pick it, listening closely to the sound. Next pick the third string. The third string should sound the same as the fourth string fingered at the fifth fret. If it sound lower, turn the third string peg to tighten it. If it sounds higher, turn third string peg to loosen it. Keep adjusting the third string until it sounds exactly the same as the fourth string fingered at the fifth fret. When the two notes sound the same, the third and fourth strings are in tune.

Follow a similar procedure for the other strings.

Finger the fourth fret of the third string. Adjust the second string up or down until it sounds the same as the third string fingered at the fourth fret.

Finger the third fret of the second string. Adjust the first string up or down until it sounds the same as the second string fingered at the third fret.

Finally, finger the fifth fret of the first string. Adjust the fifth string to sound the same as the first string fingered at the fifth fret.

If you have followed all these steps very carefully your banjo should be in tune. To test it, strum all the strings, including the fifth. That is the G chord. Does it sound good? If it does, the banjo is in tune. If the G chord sounds bad or slightly sour, one or more of the strings are still out of tune. You may have to tune several times before you get it just right. Learning to tune the banjo, like learning to play it, takes time and practice. Don't be discouraged if you don't get it right away.

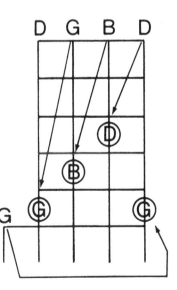

Transposing

Transposing simply means changing a song from one key to another. The keys of G and C are the easiest to play on the banjo without re-tuning. In songbooks you will find songs written in many keys. In order to accompany yourself while singing them, it will be convenient to transpose them to either G or C with the aid of this chart. For the chords in the song, simply substitute the corresponding chords in the key you're transposing to.

Remember that Bb is the same as A#, Ab is the same as G#, Gb is the same as F#, Eb is the same as D#, and Db is the same as C#.

Key	I	II	III	IV	V	VI	VII
C	C	D	E	F	G	A	B
Db	Db	Eb	F	Gb	Ab	Bb	C
D	D	E	F#	G	A	B	C#
Eb	Eb	F	G	Ab	Bb	C	D
E	E	F#	G#	A	B	C#	D#
F	F	G	A	Bb	C	D	E
Gb	Gb	Ab	Bb	Cb	Db	Eb	F
G	G	A	B	C	D	E	F#
Ab	Ab	Bb	C	Db	Eb	F	G
A	A	B	C#	D	E	F#	G#
Bb	Bb	C	D	Eb	F	G	A
B	B	C#	D#	E	F#	G#	A#

Here is a chord progression in the key of Bb transposed to the key of G.

```
G          |  E7              |  A
Bb         |  B7              |  C
↓  ↓  ↓  ↓ |  ↓  ↓  ↓  ↓      |  ↓  ↓  ↓  ↓ |

D7         |  G
F7         |  Bb
↓  ↓  ↓  ↓ |  ↓  ↓  ↓  ↓ ||
```

Here is a chord progression in the key of E transposed to the key of C.

```
C          |  Am              |  F
E          |  C#m             |  A
↓  ↓  ↓  ↓ |  ↓  ↓  ↓  ↓      |  ↓  ↓  ↓  ↓ |

G7         |  C
B7         |  E
↓  ↓  ↓  ↓ |  ↓  ↓  ↓  ↓ ||
```

The Capo

Another method of transposing involves the use of a device called a *capo.* There are several kinds of capos available, all of which perform the same function. When attached to the neck of the banjo at any fret, the capo raises the pitch of all the strings, as your first finger does when you play a bar chord. Of course the pitch of the fifth string must also be raised correspondingly. Thus, some sort of fifth string capo is required. One of the best and least expensive of these is a spring-type arm which slides on a metal track attached to the neck above the fifth fret.

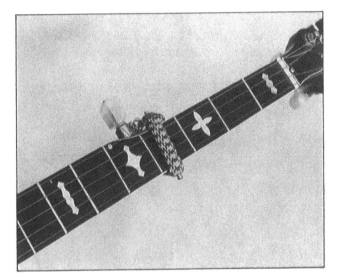

Once your banjo is properly equipped, the following chart will enable you to play in any key while fingering chords in the keys of G and C.

Place capo on fret:	I	II	III	IV	V	VI	VII
Play chords for key of G	G#/Ab	A	A#/Bb	B	C	C#/Db	D
Play chords for key of C	C#/Db	D	D#/Eb	E	F	F#/Gb	G

Going back to the chord progressions in the preceding section, you can see that, with the capo, they can be transposed back to their original keys while leaving the chords in G and C.

Chord Dictionary

The following chart will enable you to find every major, minor, and seventh chord in the open G tuning at various positions on the neck.

Fret	Major			Minor			Seventh		
I	G♯	F	C♯	Am	C♯m	Fm	G♯7	F7	C7
II	A	F♯	D	A♯m	Dm	F♯m	A7	F♯7	C♯7
III	A♯	G	D♯	Bm	D♯m	Gm	A♯7	G7	D7
IV	B	G♯	E	Cm	Em	G♯m	B7	G♯7	D♯7
V	C	A	F	C♯m	Fm	Am	C7	A7	E7
VI	C♯	A♯	F♯	Dm	F♯m	A♯m	C♯7	A♯7	F7
VII	D	B	G	D♯m	Gm	Bm	D7	B7	F♯7
VIII	D♯	C	G♯	Em	G♯m	Cm	D♯7	C7	G7
IX	E	C♯	A	Fm	Am	C♯m	E7	C♯7	G♯7
X	F	D	A♯	F♯m	A♯m	Dm	F7	D7	A7
XI	F♯	D♯	B	Gm	Bm	D♯m	F♯7	D♯7	A♯7
XII	G	E	C	G♯m	Cm	Em	G7	E7	B7
XIII	G♯	F	C♯	Am	C♯m	Fm	G♯m	F7	C7
Etc.									

Other Tunings

There are many other tunings for the banjo with which you should become familiar. Particularly useful are: *Standard C, G Modal, Double C,* and *Open D.* For study of these and other tunings see Art Rosenbaum's *Old-Time Mountain Banjo,* and Pete Seeger's *How to Play the Five-String Banjo,* both available from Oak Publications.

Parts of the Banjo

Playing Condition

Nothing is more frustrating than trying to play on a defective banjo. You don't need an expensive instrument. A cheaper one will do just fine, but it has to be in playable condition. Have your teacher check it over. Even brand-new banjos often need minor adjustments before they're ready to be played, but leave the work to someone qualified to do it.

Use the following checklist to determine the playing condition of your banjo.

1) The head should be tight, not loose or sagging.
2) The neck should be straight, not warped or bowed.
3) The strings should not be too far from the frets. If they are they will be too hard to press down.
4) The strings should not be too close to the frets. If they are they will buzz against the frets when you pick them.
5) The bridge should be correctly positioned. If it isn't the strings cannot be accurately tuned.
6) The strings should be in good condition. If they are old and rusted they should be replaced with a new set of light gauge strings.

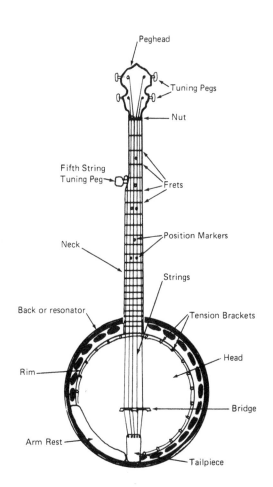

Glossary

Accompaniment— A rhythmic instrumental background for singing.

Bar— The placing of one finger across more than one string.

Bluegrass— A style of country music developed by Bill Monroe, taking its name from his group, the Blue Grass Boys. Three-finger banjo picking.

Capo— A clamp device attached to the neck of a fretted instrument to raise the pitch of all the strings uniformly.

Chord— Three or more different notes sounded simultaneously.

Clawhammer— A melodic form of frailing, using few strums and much drop-thumbing.

Double-thumbing— A variation of the frailing rhythm in which the thumb picks the fifth string twice.

Drop-thumbing— Another variation of the frailing rhythm in which the thumb picks notes on the inside strings.

Frailing— An Appalachian banjo style characterized by downward finger strokes of the right hand.

Fret— A metal strip set into the fingerboard of a stringed instrument against which the strings are pressed.

Key— A piece is said to be in a certain key when the chords and notes seem to revolve around the main note. For example, the chords C, F and G all seem to revolve around the note C— the first note of the C major scale. A key can often be figured out by the last note or chord of a piece.

Lick— A short musical phrase.

Open G Tuning— Tuning the strings to the notes of a G chord — GDGBD.

Open String— A string played without being fretted by the left hand.

Roll— In bluegrass playing, a pattern of notes picked by the right hand fingers.

Rhythm— The regular, recurring beat or pulse of a musical composition.

Scruggs-picking— The bluegrass banjo style developed by Earl Scruggs.

Strum— Sounding the strings with a brushing motion of the right hand, as opposed to picking them individually.

Tablature— A system of musical notation for fretted instruments which shows the strings as lines and the frets as numbers.

Tag Ending— A short phrase played after the musical end of a piece. The tag used most often in country music is the familiar ''shave and a haircut—two bits.''

Transposing— Changing a tune from one key to another.

Up-picking— A banjo style, similar to frailing, in which the melody notes are picked in an upward direction.

Discography

To develop your feeling for banjo music and to improve your playing there's nothing like listening to live music and playing with other musicians. The next best thing is to study the music from records. The following albums represent a good cross-section of the many styles of five-string banjo playing.

American Banjo: Scruggs Style - Folkways FA-2314B

Clawhammer Banjo - County 701

Folk Banjo Styles - Electra EKL-7217

More Clawhammer Banjo - County 717

Music of Roscoe Holcomb & Wade Ward - Folkways FA-2363

Old-Time Banjo Project - Electra EKS-7276

Old-Timers from the Grand Ole Opry - Folkways FA-2379

New Dimensions in Banjo and Bluegrass - Electra EKS-7238

Will the Circle be Unbroken - United Artists 9801

Bibliography

The following books will provide you with enough material to keep you busy for months. They are all excellent.

Clawhammer Banjo, by Miles Krassen (Oak)

Bluegrass Banjo, by Peter Wernick (Oak)

Bluegrass Songbook, by Peter Wernick (Oak)

Folksinger's Wordbook, by Irwin Silber (Oak)

Folk Music Sourcebook, by Sandberg & Weisman (Oak)

How to Play the Five-String Banjo, by Pete Seeger (Oak)

John Burke's Book of Old-Time Fiddle Tunes for Banjo, (Amsco)

Melodic Banjo, by Tony Trishka (Oak)

Old-Time Mountain Banjo, by Art Rosenbaum (Oak)